Who's To Say
Cats Don't Praise!

BREN GANDY-WILSON

*"Let everything that has breath
  praise the LORD!"*
Psalm 150:6

WestBow
P R E S S
A DIVISION OF THOMAS NELSON

WestBow Press books may be ordered through booksellers or by contacting:

WestBow Press
A Division of Thomas Nelson
1663 Liberty Drive
Bloomington, IN 47403
www.westbowpress.com
1-(866) 928-1240

Because of the dynamic nature of the Internet, any web addresses or links contained in
this book may have changed since publication and may no longer be valid. The views
expressed in this work are solely those of the author and do not necessarily reflect the
views of the publisher, and the publisher hereby disclaims any responsibility for them.

Any people depicted in stock imagery provided by Thinkstock are models,
and such images are being used for illustrative purposes only.
Certain stock imagery © Thinkstock.

Illustrations by:
Lency Donnell August contributed the cover photo and several pieces of art. He also
contributed pieces for the author's first book, "Women are Spiritual BRIDGES."

Lafayette Gould is an accomplished artist who has done extensive art
work before contributing to "Who's To Say Cats Don't Praise!"

ISBN: 978-1-4497-7929-0 (sc)
ISBN: 978-1-4497-7930-6 (e)

Library of Congress Control Number: 2012923498

All Scriptural quotations are taken from the Holy Bible, Life
Application Study, International Or Amplified.

Printed in the United States of America

WestBow Press rev. date: 1/7/2013

Dedicated to the Rockingham Animal Shelter; a local branch of the Society for the Prevention of Cruelty to Animals (SPCA), Rockingham, North Carolina.

Also, a shout out to my brother Robin, perhaps the greatest animal trainer of all time!

Introduction

I believe it is safe to say that most pet owners feel a special bond with their animal companions. A recent estimate of pet owners in the United States shows that about 55 million people have dogs and about 60 million have cats. Animal companions become important family members for both people living alone as well as for people with children and spouses. There are even many homeless people who take in a stray animal to care for. Animals serve as nurturers in our busy society, giving us the attention and contact we need. Let's not forget the true meaning of "pet" is to touch or caress. Source: Delta Society (www.deltasociety.org)

A pet is always there to receive comfort, listen to you and to talk to when needed. Their ability to help people go through difficult times by providing emotional support through just being there is well known.

There are multiple cases where pets have helped people with physical ailments such as dogs detecting cancer and imminent seizures. Animals have also been shown to help people cope with emotional troubles like depression; and pets have improved the quality of life for people in nursing homes; giving them a reason for hope and a will to continue living. People with pets are much less likely to be stubborn and uncooperative when it comes to taking their medications and getting out of bed to exercise.

Several medical reports have credited animals with positive effects on people's lives such as:

- Lowering blood pressure and stress for everyday people
- Helping people cope with the loss of a loved one and other major life changes
- Better communication in marriages
- Service animals like seeing-eye dogs help people with disabilities live normal lives
- Helping people cope with cancer, Alzheimer's and AIDS
- Higher survival rates for people with coronary heart disease
- Better socialization of young children with peers and development of nurturing behavior
- Giving a sense of constancy to foster children
- Improving treatment results for anxious and depressed people
- Therapeutic horseback riding has helped improve balance, posture, mobility, language, and muscle coordination
- Helping facilitate social interactions between strangers and improving social behavior for mentally impaired people and prisoners.
- Increases recreational activity such as dog walking

There are many remarkable stories of animals that heal people. Many animals, from dogs and cats to rabbits, llamas, dolphins, and horses, have played a role in the healing process.

Not all animal companions cause people to heal completely; but their being there does help boost people's attitudes and encourage them to live their lives to the fullest.

One cold, icy wet day, while walking home
through the park, Ersa spotted a feral
kitty cat shivering under a bush.

Her heart went out as she slowly stooped to take a closer look. Without thinking, she reached out and gathered the kitty cat close. *"Don't worry little one,"* she cooed. *"I'll take care of you."*

Ersa was concerned that if she didn't bring the kitty cat home, it wouldn't last one more day in the icy cold weather. She carefully tucked the kitty cat under her coat; and slowly walked home with kitty gathered close to her bosom.

As she walked, she thought about what trials the kitty cat might have endured during its wilderness wanderings?

Perhaps it had been out in the weather for quite some time.

Had it been chased by vicious dogs?

Did the kitty cat yearn for a warm cozy rug in front of a roaring fire place?

The kitty cat was not wearing any tags, and there were no tell-tale signs that there had ever been a collar around its neck.

So Ersa decided to bring the kitty cat home while visions of playing, laughing and frolicking flooded her head.

During the walk home, the kitty cat relaxed against Ersa's warm heartbeat.

But to her dismay, she was met with total silence when she opened her coat to reveal a tiny sleeping ball of fur.

Her happy smile faded away as she heard her husband Angus say, *"Get rid of it!"* Ersa withered under his gaze as she desperately searched for a way out.

She glanced out the window as the icy rain continued to fall. She felt the damp fur shiver. *"How could she send it back out into that?"* she thought.

She also knew they might put it to sleep if she took it to a shelter.

Reasoning did no good; tears only made things worse. Ersa knew matters were grave when an ultimatum he gave. Her heart sank to her knees as she heard Angus say, *"Either it goes or I will!"*

Under her husband's icy gaze, Ersa tried
to reason. *"As soon as winter's over,"* she
pleaded. Angus' eyes met hers with
suspicion. But to her surprise, he silently
turned aside.

But a temporary reprieve soon melted from her heart; as a good, old-fashioned deadlock was wrought.

Winter moved inside that day.

In the meanwhile, the kitty cat slept and ate and relaxed as it roamed around its new home. It had a cute, furry face with busy little hands and feet that darted around as fast as its swishing little tail.

Late one Saturday morning, Ersa slowly
made her way downstairs. She had
languished in bed much longer than usual.
Suddenly, she thought about the kitty cat!
It was totally alone with Angus!

She rushed into the den just in time to see the kitty cat heading towards Angus. Before she could say, *"No! Don't do that!"* The kitty cat purred softly and began rubbing its body against Angus' leg.

But to her surprise, rather than jerking his leg away, Angus reached down gingerly and placed the kitty cat on his lap!

When he realized Ersa was standing in the room, *"Would you like to know why I reacted so strongly when you brought this little one home?"* He said. *"Certainly,"* Ersa said, not daring to breathe.

Ersa learned a side of her husband she might never have known if the kitty cat had not entered their lives that fateful day.

It was a story Angus had chosen to bury years ago.

From a baby up until he was about 11
years old, little Angus had owned a cat he
called Callie. Callie had been a constant
friend to a shy little boy after his father
went away. Because of Callie, little Angus
was not afraid to stay alone while his
mother worked in the evenings.

But things changed forever when his
mother married a man who hated cats.
"Just another mouth to feed, and too much fur!"
said he. *"Either it goes or I will,"* he told
little Angus' mother one day.

Mother looked sad but said nothing. Later, she hugged little Angus helplessly and told him in private not to worry. Let her try to reason with her new husband.

Little Angus watched sadly as the once sunny environment in his home changed to cloudy with a chance of rain.

"What an awful weight for a little boy to bear," Ersa thought.

Finally, little Angus could take it no
more. He didn't like seeing his mother
so unhappy. That day he decided to take
Callie away so his mother wouldn't be
sad any more. He didn't know then what
might happen at a shelter.

Little Angus' spirit was broken and he
vowed he would never love that way again.

From that time on, he became a behavior problem at school. He isolated himself, preferring to be alone. *"Giving my cat away changed me. I was mad and I was hurt, and I wanted to hurt back. The issues I dealt with were never the issues that caused my pain."*

"As a teenager, I dropped out of school and joined the Peace Corps. From there, I enlisted in the Army."

Ersa just listened as tears silently trickled down her face. She felt only sorrow for a little boy whose heart had been broken so long ago.

She quickly moved to sit beside Angus. They both stroked the kitty cat and she became *"Callie"* that day.

Angus laughed as he stroked Callie. *"This little girl and I have been getting more and more acquainted every day. Through the silence of watching her and the persistence of her love and affection, I begin to remember my real issue. It was the loss of my best friend that caused my real pain! With recognition, I am beginning to heal."*

Ersa gently punched Angus on the shoulder. *"You're not so tough after all, Mister,"* she said. *"Yeah, you're right, but don't tell anybody."* They both laughed.

"But seriously though, I know I have been a horrible, dominating and verbally abusive husband. I am ready now to take full responsibility for the wrong emotional response I made all those years ago. I don't want my past to keep ruining my future. Will you forgive me?"

Ersa moved to embrace her husband. The love for him that shone in her eyes needed no words.

A greater bond of trust, love and compassion had come through Callie as visions of playing, frolicking and laughter became real at the Jenkins's home that day.

So, who *is* to say cats don't praise!

Let everything that hath breath praise the LORD - All living things in the air, the earth, and the waters. Let there be one universal burst of praise. Let His praises be celebrated not only with instruments of music, but let all living beings unite in that praise; let a breathing universe combine in one solemn service of praise!

Printed in the United States
By Bookmasters